Alice Turton

Gerhard
A Love Story

Gerhard

A Love Story

Betty Kennedy

Macmillan of Canada/Toronto

ISBN 0-7705-1411-1

Printed in Canada for
The Macmillan Company of Canada
70 Bond Street, Toronto M5B 1X3

FOR GERHARD

CONTENTS

Bermuda

THE fine part about Bermuda is that your holiday begins the moment you step off the plane. There it is, the sea. And here somehow it is the sea at its best, colours almost unreal in their beauty, breakers that race to a foamy finale, then gentle their way back out to the whole to build again. Perhaps it is that eternal quality of the sea that holds us, that paradox of changelessness and constant change.

We walk from the plane across the tarmac,

Gerhard with his arm hugging me. Our daughter Tracy, twelve, and Mildred, more like a sister than my aunt, walk on either side of us. It is our ninth holiday in Bermuda, and this is to be the best yet because we have two full weeks instead of the usual ten days. In past years we have come down with another couple. This year, however, it is strictly family. Gerhard, who is naturally far more gregarious than I am, says he is glad. He will have me all to himself.

There is scurrying about and laughter in organizing golf bags, baggage, and counting the pieces into the taxi, and then we are driving in the sunshine, along the South Shore Road to the small house we rent, year after year, and to the familiar faces of the people who run the cottage colony. We are greeted as long-time friends with hugs and exclamations; they even know that my husband's name is pronounced "Gerrard", with the stress on the second syllable.

There are flowers in our house, and the look from our living room out across the sea hasn't changed. The whispering pines outside our front door still frame the spectacular view. The hibiscus hedge at the back still displays its opulent red blooms, and the air still has that unbelievable, clean, moist, caressing feel.

In something less than an hour we are unpacked, have our motorbikes ready to go, and are off to Hamilton to grocery shop. Tracy rides on the back of my bike and Mildred on the back of Gerhard's. With Gerhard, even grocery shopping is an adventure. He knows the butcher, by name, and they have a great conference about meat cuts and prices, and about what's happened since last year and the state of the world in general, while I do the rest of the shopping.

How can I describe what those Bermuda days were like? That island was for us not just a place, but a time-out of any and all pressures of ordinary living. Like the time you spend wading a trout stream. Or on the golf course, when your entire concentration is on one specific thing and there is nothing more important than that next shot, or the look of a particular hole with its soul-satisfying pattern of grass, trees, sea, and sky.

For the next two weeks our lives slipped into the idyllic Bermuda rhythm we had grown into over the years. Gerhard and I, who always waken early, enjoy riding our bikes along the spectacular South Shore Road about 7:30 a.m., cut up over the hill to Riddell's Bay, and are on the golf course before eight. We play as many holes as we can in about an hour and a half, picking and choosing different ones each day on the still-quiet course, then ride back to the cottage for breakfast at ten with Tracy and Mil. Evelyn, the maid, comes in each morning to do breakfast and clean. She has looked after us every year, and we always exchange family news.

Beach time, shopping expeditions, bike trips all over the island exploring winding roads we haven't been over before fill our days. Gerhard and I do the cooking, as we always do together at home. There are just a few people to see, as we deliberately keep our Bermuda time free.

There's Mr. Hughes of the twangy Boston accent, a commercial fisherman who took some time to lose his suspicion of Gerhard and to discover that he really didn't want anything from him, just to learn a bit about his life. Gerhard always goes by for a long chat with him about his work and the state of the fishing. Some years he takes him a book or some little something he thinks will please Mr. Hughes. This year Gerhard is annoyed with himself. He had intended to bring Mr. Hughes a certain kind of wire he once said he had trouble getting. Mr. Hughes would be somewhat puzzled and surprised if he knew of Gerhard's chagrin with himself; he would probably never even remember having mentioned the wire last year.

Then there is Mrs. Dorothy Maconachie, Brigadier Maconachie's widow, whom we have over for breakfast. That acquaintance tells something about my husband. The property next to where we stay is a large and beautiful estate, and Gerhard sought out Brigadier Maconachie one morning just to tell him how much he admired his place. The Brigadier not only spent several hours showing him around, he got out architect's drawings and plans to show what he hoped to accomplish with the land in future. I can just visualize the mounting excitement of that conversation as Gerhard brought his exuberant imagination to the Brigadier's plans. Gerhard had that rare gift of making you believe all things were possible. If you wanted to do something, all you had to do was talk to Gerhard about it and you came away firmly believing you *could* do it — and with several good ideas from him to boot.

Our Bermuda days are full, happy ones, but this year there is one difference. Gerhard, who is always ready with a new foray in mind, now tires easily. Five or six holes of golf in the morning is about all we get through, instead of eight or nine. The bike rides leave him obviously uncomfortable, although he doesn't complain. I'm concerned about him. I wanted him to have a medical check-up in Toronto before we came away, but he was insistent that after our holiday would be soon enough.

The two weeks are gone all too quickly. When it is time to leave, I have a feeling of unutterable sadness, a feeling that we have had our last holiday in Bermuda, although I can't explain the emotion. Perhaps it's just that I always hate to let go of precious moments, knowing they never do come again. Like the feeling you have when you close up the cottage at the end of summer. Leaving Bermuda this time gives me that hollow-in-the-pit-of-the-stomach feeling. And somehow there isn't all the usual talk about what we'll do here next year.

Doctors

IN that first week back in Toronto we immersed ourselves in our business lives. After careers in the fashion industry and in film-making, Gerhard had plunged into the challenges and frustrations of the comparatively new business of air-supported enclosures for industrial, warehouse, and recreational uses, while I was busy in my familiar world of broadcasting with my radio show for CFRB and "Front Page Challenge" for the CBC.

But even with his healthful-looking Bermuda

tan, Gerhard was not his energetic self. After I had repeatedly suggested he see David Smith, our family doctor, he finally snapped at me, "I don't need David to tell me I've got cancer of the bowel. That can wait until next week. I have too many things I must do."

I pointed out the logic of either removing that fear if it was unfounded, or immediately tackling the problem if he did have cancer. He changed the subject, but we both knew the problem was there, still unresolved.

Because I was now determined to get Gerhard to the doctor as soon as possible, I put in a call to David. I found that Gerhard had called to make an appointment earlier that same day.

David diagnosed a tumor of the bowel, just as Gerhard had thought. David then called in Dr. Bryce Taylor for a more detailed diagnosis. A round of tests followed; we were to have some more definite word in a couple of days.

The day we are to hear the verdict turns out to be the day we have invited several guests for dinner. My mind is in a turmoil. I want to call our friends and cancel. Gerhard will not hear of it. "If I am really for it, cancelling a dinner isn't going to do anything for anybody. We've looked forward to this evening. Let's enjoy it."

We go together to the appointment with Dr. Taylor, and sit opposite him, holding hands. Gerhard's younger brother, Bill, who has always been close to him and who has been through the torment of his own son's battle with Hodgkin's disease, has come for the appointment too.

Dr. Taylor begins by asking if he should speak freely, since after all it is Gerhard's medical problem that he will be outlining. Gerhard says simply, "There are no secrets here. There is nothing about me that Betty shouldn't know, and my brother Bill can hear anything you have to say."

Dr. Taylor explains the situation in a cool, detached way, and even draws a diagram to show graphically where the tumor is. Gerhard humorously expresses the hope that his surgical skills are better than his artistic ones and begins asking questions.

The tumor is malignant. To remove it can mean a colostomy, though they will not know that for sure until they get in there. Dr. Taylor explains that he would be working on the operation with Dr. Bob Wilkinson. With considerable wisdom, Dr. Taylor, who is quite a lot younger than my husband, says, "I can just imagine what it's like to sit there and listen to me. I'm younger than you are. You must wonder. It's a serious operation; if I were in your place I would want another opinion." He suggested

Gerhard might want to talk to Dr. Wilkinson, or to someone else of his choice.

At no time did Dr. Taylor minimize the dangers, but he did give us hope that surgery could be successful. He was factual with us, and honest, and we were both well enough informed to appreciate how serious things were. One other point: he believed that the tumor had been there for a long time. Clearly, there was no point in feeling any guilt about having taken the Bermuda vacation when we did, for at that stage a couple of weeks would have made no difference.

I came out of that office in a state of shock, though Gerhard appeared calm and as much in control as ever. His concern was for me, his reassurances, his comforting, for me. We all three began talking about the hopeful aspects. Bill, a veteran of countless visits to Princess Margaret Hospital with his young son, now recovered from Hodgkin's and back at university, was supportive and encouraging. He recommended we talk to Dr. Walter Rider at Princess Margaret. A doctor friend of Bill's had told him that he personally would never undergo any surgery for cancer without first consulting Dr. Rider, who was getting good results with radiation.

We decided that I would call Dr. Rider and ask him to see Gerhard. In the meantime, Gerhard was to be booked into the hospital within the next few days for further tests — and surgery, if that proved to be the necessary route.

That same evening our friends did come to dinner. One couple came with a houseguest of theirs, an attractive woman who had been recently widowed. Her warm and affectionate letter of thanks for what she called the most pleasant evening in many months made me realize that Gerhard was right. Whatever was ahead, we must try to live our lives as fully as always. Curious that we should have had anything to offer that guest at a time when our own lives were being torn from their moorings.

Dr. Rider was approachable and sympathetic on the phone, and more than a little intrigued with who Gerhard Kennedy was, since my call was the third one about him. Dr. Taylor and Dr. David Smith had also called him. His specialty was radiation, and he favoured that approach to the tumor problem if surgery was going to mean a colostomy. If surgery did *not* mean a colostomy he felt it would be a good solution.

Gerhard was now in Western Hospital and we were faced with two different approaches to the problem. If Gerhard were to choose surgery, the operation would be the following day. He had talks with Dr. Taylor, with our family physician Dr.

11

David Smith, with Dr. Wilkinson, and with Dr. Rider. Each man brought to the discussion his individual expertise and opinion. The surgeons frankly admitted they were familiar with surgical solutions, while the radiation specialist made it clear that he was more familar with results from radiation.

Gerhard and I spent several hours talking about the best course to follow. While he found the idea of a colostomy offensive, he could have accepted it if it were clearly the only avenue open to him. Surgery did not frighten him. The elements he weighed in the argument were these: surgery, he believed, would require a recovery period of a month to three months, providing all went well. If the cancer proved to be more extensive than we hoped, surgery might only deprive him of his strength for precious weeks when he had so much he wanted to do. There were no guarantees that either surgery or radiation could offer a permanent solution, so he had to think in terms of time.

The final advice from the doctors involved was for Gerhard to follow his own gut-feeling. Gerhard chose the radiation route, fully aware it was not the conventional one, but hoping that it offered him the better chance. So it was with a sense of relief and guarded optimism that he checked out of the hospital. We had been home from our Bermuda holiday for only two weeks; but our world was now a vastly different one.

Treatment

FROM the first, Gerhard was open and direct about the cancer. Our children, Mark, Shawn, D'Arcy, all young men now in their twenties, and Tracy, our twelve-year-old daughter, knew as much about what was going on as we did ourselves. And certainly we let his children by his first marriage know and Agnes, his former wife.

Gerhard, with his energetic natural approach to life, was cheerful, hard at work every day, living each day exactly as he would have under other circumstances. For my part, I felt as though I were operating on automatic pilot. I went through the motions, did things expected of me, but much of me was somewhere else in an empty world of panic.

On April 15, 1975, I had promised to go to Ottawa with a delegation making a presentation to Justice Minister Otto Lang in favour of the abolition of the death penalty. The commitment had been made well in advance. Knowing I was going to be in Ottawa, I had also dropped a personal note to Mrs. Trudeau inviting her to luncheon. She had accepted. An interview with the Ambassador of the People's Republic of China and one with the official Commissioner of Bilingualism, Keith Spicer, completed the Ottawa schedule for the day. I was for cancelling out the whole thing but Gerhard persuaded me to go. He insisted on life-as-usual, enjoy every single minute, not only for himself but for me and the family.

In the early daylight hours of that day, I kissed him as he lay sleeping beside me and put this note beside him.

Very Early Tuesday Morning

Darling Man:

A special little "I love you" till this evening. I begrudge even the few hours away from you to go to Ottawa. The best part of the whole day will be getting back here to share it with you.

Have you any idea my darling how special you make life for me? You are most of life for me . . . . lover, husband, father of our children, dearest friend, and companion. Nothing will ever change that.

Will phone you during the day and see you tonight.

All my love always.
Bett.

Dr. Rider embarked on a series of tests and out of these a program of radiation was planned with Gerhard. The program called for five weeks of radiation treatment: one a day, five days a week, for five weeks. And then we would see where we were.

I went with Gerhard to see how these treatments were done. As he had always done with everything around him, Gerhard asked questions, wanted explanations, wanted to know what was happening and why.

We had been warned that the treatments could be quite debilitating. When you think about it, rays strong enough to kill off cells are bound to have some effect on the total person. For Gerhard there was the feeling that he was burned inside, and the exhaustion which he fought so valiantly that he did not miss one day of work in the months that followed. There were days, though, when he had to come limping home by three-thirty or four to stretch out for "half an hour"; the half-hour often turned into an hour or two.

Even then, as soon as I came in the door he would get up and come into the kitchen for our normal ritual of getting the family dinner together. You couldn't shoo him out, suggest he stretch out in the living room, for the answer was always a cheerful "I want to be here with you."

All May and into early June, the treatments continued. Our life was the full, rich one of sharing it had been for twenty-eight years, but now there was a painful poignancy to so many moments. When I watched Gerhard feed the cardinal who came cheekily to our bedroom window every morning; when I stood behind him, arms around his middle, kissing his bare back and shoulders as he shaved. At times like these tears would often come unbidden.

Our life has not been always smooth, without problems; we have suffered reverses, disappointments, failures. But the one constant thing has been our feeling for each other. There has not been a morning in our lives together when we did not waken in one another's arms, or reach out for each other and say, "I love you." That is quite literally true. Yet there was nothing mundane or routine about the words, always a sense of wonder in what we knew in each other. I honestly don't know why we were so blessed. I only know we were.

And then, miraculously, comes a period in which we believe that Gerhard is growing stronger. It's sometimes five o'clock, then six o'clock before he has to lie down for an hour. He looks surprisingly well, considering the cancer he is battling. And we are so hopeful.

We are playing as much golf as possible. Gerhard loves the game and understands it as few people do. We play a few holes each day after work. Sometimes three or four. Sometimes just one or two. If Gerhard becomes too uncomfortable he will sometimes ride the cart and watch me play, coaching each shot. And if I suggest packing it up he says he would rather be uncomfortable out on the golf course watching me than someplace else.

The people at the club know Gerhard has cancer, and on weekends, his golfing friends, particularly the Manns and Valdes, are considerate in seeking games and understanding if we cannot go the round, even with a cart.

The radiation treatments stop, then they are

resumed, but not on a daily basis. They still leave Gerhard drained, but undiminished in spirit. Dr. Rider is surprised that he continues to work every day, let alone play some golf. He does not know my beloved and his capacity for life. If believing you are going to get well can make you well, Gerhard will have it made.

Somehow, from somewhere, he draws the strength not only to take Tracy to her riding classes, but to show enthusiasm and encouragement to each of us in our many endeavours. He watches D'Arcy practise his golf and gives him pointers that are useful and well considered. He makes a point of watching certain sports on TV so that he can share that interest with Mark, our oldest son, whose other abiding interest, philosophy, doesn't provide much meeting ground for them.

As if to point up Gerhard's own battle, during these weeks now death takes its toll of our friends. Within a very short space of time we lose our long-time friend and almost retired family physician Arthur Smith, David's father; Winks Cran who was President of CFRB, and infinitely more to us than a business associate; Jack Dennett, who together with his wife Norma had shared one of those time-out-of-reality Bermuda vacations; and Stephen Wildridge, the twenty-five-year-old artist, son of Jennie and Jack, killed instantly in an auto accident. It is as though death is all around us.

We saw Jack and Norma many times during the last weeks of his life, making the long drive from our home in the west end clear across town to the hospital in Scarborough. Jack, too, had cancer, and in some strange way I think he felt that was a bond with Gerhard, a bond that drew them even closer than their old friendship. Tired as Gerhard often was in the evening, he would be determined to go to see Jack, and would spend time dreaming up tempting little treats for a failing appetite. We were both so fond of Jack, his death was particularly hard to bear; and Gerhard ruefully wondered aloud if he would go in the same way.

For the first time we began, seriously, to face the possibility out loud that the cancer might finally win.

Vacation

WE began, early in July, to talk of our vacation plans. Much of the early part of the summer seemed like time suspended because of Gerhard's treatments, but now we felt we should make some plans. Gerhard was still mobile, and while he had some pretty bad days, he was still working.

Our friends the Rosses had given us an open-ended invitation to their place on Lake Superior. We had visited them in earlier years and, from their place, had launched on a camping expedition along the North Shore. That trip two years previously had been one of the memorable adventures of our lifetime as Gerhard had taken us exploring the splendours of that wilderness shore. What a time of discovery that was, and how many memories we have of that trip.

We swam those icy waters, fished the streams that fed the lake, enjoyed the mystery of what lay round the next bend in the shoreline. And we collected so many beautiful rocks we finally had to do a sort-and-discard job in the interest of safety on the homeward trip in our small boat. One of the trip's real treasures is a fossil I found; a solitary horn coral that dates back to 450 million years B.C., according to Royal Ontario Museum authorities. Gerhard had it mounted in a ring for me; it has more meaning than any rare jewel could ever have.

But the ruggedness of Lake Superior's northern shore could not be for us this summer of '75 — though what Gerhard wanted to do sounded almost as strenuous. He wanted to show Tracy the mountains of the West Coast and and to visit Shawn, our son, who was living with Beverly in the mountains north and west of Lillooet.

And so we made our plans: we'd fly to Vancouver, spend a few days with Nancy, Gerhard's daughter; then we'd drive to where Shawn and Beverly were living and spend a couple of weeks with them. On our return trip we'd see our friends Evan and Roy Mackie in Victoria, the Carnats in Calgary, show Tracy Banff, and see the Ian Mackies there. Tracy and Gerhard would fly home for school opening, while I remained in Calgary to do the two opening "Front Page Challenge" shows of the new season on September 1. I'd fly home the next day.

It was a typical Gerhard venture. He even wondered aloud just where our friends Alan and Ruth Collier would be and if we might not arrange to rendezvous with them someplace. That sounded a little impractical, and even without that it was an ambitious plan.

As the dates drew closer I wondered about the advisability of going. When I suggested that we might better bring Shawn and Beverly east to see us, that didn't satisfy Gerhard. He insisted we go ahead as planned. We could always cancel out if the going got too tough.

And go we did.

Gerhard had the pleasure of showing Tracy the mountains and the lovely look of Vancouver. He did some business there and we had the fun of Stanley Park and the aquarium, an extra-special Chinese dinner with Nancy, and shopping for supplies for

Shawn and Beverly. We were set to drive our rented car to Gold Bridge and then to Tyaughton Lake.

You would have to understand that Gerhard always drove a car as easily and effortlessly as most of us breathe. He was at home, relaxed, and comfortable in a car, and so observant it was always he who saw the hawk circling, the groundhog darting into a hole, the flower or plant that was new to him, or the unusual bird he would later identify in a bird guide. So on that drive from Vancouver when Gerhard asked me to do some of the driving, I knew he was feeling awful.

With a pillow and a light blanket he made himself comfortable in the back seat and slept for a time. After an overnight in Lillooet he felt able to drive again, and no one enjoyed more than he the spectacular view from some of the roads, the path the river carved into the mountains, and the thrill of seeing a great bald eagle.

We spent four days with Shawn and Beverly, visiting in their snug cabin a few feet from the water's edge on a beautiful mountain lake. We fished a nearby mountain stream and Gerhard caught the most trout. We picked vivid blue delphiniums that grew profusely in a field, and watched and photographed a mother osprey and her two young, wheeling and flying back and forth from a nest.

But the toll all this was taking of Gerhard was becoming increasingly visible. When fishing a stream, which he so dearly loved and did so expertly, he would now have to take a break and lie down in the car after every twenty minutes or so.

When I suggested to him on that fourth day that we had seen Shawn, had shown Tracy the mountains, now didn't he think we should just head for home, he agreed. And it was I, who have such an unreasoning fear of heights, who drove most of those mountain roads back to Vancouver. My darling, whose loving shelter and protective strength had always been there like a rock, a base for my very existence, was slowly, surely losing that strength. And all I could do was offer him whatever there was of me.

There was a nightmarish quality about that trip home. Difficulty in getting reservations, a rude and obnoxious young man at the seat assignment desk, and finally seats aboard the aircraft smack up against the movie screen and with two young children directly behind Gerhard continually kicking the back of his seat. The flight seemed endless. I felt frantic for him. He remained calm and full of reassurance for me and Tracy.

To be home and in our own bed was an enormous relief. We even dared hope the pain would go away and Gerhard might again be making progress.

But the pain didn't go away, and this time it was high in the abdomen and chest. Gerhard was growing short of breath, and began to wonder if his heart was acting up, or if there was cancer all through him. Strangely, he did not fall prey to the terrible depressions we had been warned about, though he did have bouts of irritability when he was cross and crotchety. And once his awareness of the cancer's effect on his memory made him weep with frustration. But in the main it was Gerhard who kept our spirits up, and not the other way around.

At this point Dr. Rider was out of town, but an appointment was made with another doctor. He was noncommital on most things except that we had done the right thing in coming home. He ordered more tests and told us as gently as possible that the liver might now be affected.

My mind grows hazy about those next days. Appointments and tests run together in a confused pattern. But I know all too clearly I had to go back west to Calgary to do "Front Page Challenge" on the same day that Gerhard was to have the tests' results.

The clock never ticked so slowly. Finally at three o'clock Calgary time I phoned. Gerhard sounded strong and vibrant and cheerful. When I asked about the results he said there was some hitch, they had to be double-checked and wouldn't be ready until the following day. And because I wanted to believe there was just a delay and there could still be good news, I didn't press him too much. In the back of my mind was the fear that he was reluctant to tell me the results.

As always when I was out-of-town overnight, I called again after the shows, to share the experiences of the evening and say a goodnight "I love you". And then Gerhard sounded terribly tired, almost anxious to end our conversation. I was coming back the next day and he promised to be at the airport to meet me.

And he was . . . so dear and handsome in his new beige gaberdine suit, bought only a couple weeks before to fit the trimmer lines the weight loss had left him.

Even after all these years my heart still turns over when I see Gerhard after any kind of absence. I have never met any other person in my entire life with the power to kindle such excitement in me. He embraces life so fully, with such energy, with a love of everything living, with insatiable curiosity, and a tenderness and compassion that can only come from strength.

For me he makes everything possible: it's not only that he does a thousand and one thoughtful things for me and our family, it's that he makes me a thoughtful person and a person of unlimited possibilities.

Oddly, the beige suit is very like the one he was wearing the first time I ever saw him, across a room at a party in Montreal. While I was asking my friends the Collyers who he was, I could see him asking someone to bring him over and introduce us. He came back to me three times in the next half-hour to be sure I would be at the Normandy Roof later with my friends. He had a dinner engagement but would come looking for me as soon as dinner was over.

He took me home that evening, and from then on there was no other person for either of us, though our early life was far from easily organized. Some years later when we saw "South Pacific" on Broadway, the lyrics of "Some Enchanted Evening", sounded as though they had been written about us.

Looking at him now at the top of the stairs in the airport I am anxious for the good feeling of his arms around me. We tell each other our *I love yous* and how long the hours have seemed. He asks about the shows, the flight, as we move through the crowds and I have to interrupt. I can't wait any longer. *What is the news of the tests?* Gerhard stops, puts both arms around me and, with a wry smile, says, "The news is all bad. All bad."

"Oh my darling. My dearest beloved darling." And the tears spill over. Gerhard holds me close as other travellers stream past and tells me he has known since Monday, but could not give me such a verdict on the phone when I was alone and away from home with work ahead of me. Our children and Glen, my stepdaughter, a dear friend, all know the news.

He says the hardest thing in his life was not hearing the finality of the doctor's words, but in having to tell me. He feels as though he is letting me down, running out on me.

We begin the drive home from the airport and through my tears we talk it out. There is no mistake: the cancer has spread to the liver, and that will be fatal. There are no answers through surgery. The doctor has suggested that Gerhard get his affairs in order. He either will not, or truthfully cannot, give him an estimate of how much time he will have. When Gerhard asked our family doctor if it would likely be days, weeks, or months, the answer was "probably months".

Once, early in our courtship, I had described Gerhard to my parents as the kind of person who could be told the world was going to end tomorrow and who would say, "Well . . . then . . . let's see . . . . Here's what we'll do till then." Crazy how I should have spoken words like that. They were almost prophetic.

Search

IN the days and nights that followed that awful September day, it was I who cried. And it was Gerhard, in the privacy of our bed, who held me, comforted me, stroked me, told me to cry it all out while he was there with me. When I sobbed that I should be doing the comforting and not be upsetting him he only said, "Who would want to end their life and have no one to shed a tear for them? Cry all you want, my darling. That's what I'm here for, to look after you."

We always had been able to talk to one another, and that was more important than ever now. Gerhard recalled how in the beginnings of our life together he had had qualms about the difference in our ages. I remembered well his concerns about the fourteen years between us. But, at that time, I had naively connected them with superficial appearances only. Gerhard, however, had been foreseeing the distinct possibility that his lifetime would not last mine.

Not once did my husband lapse into anything remotely resembling self-pity or bitterness. He talked to me patiently, calmly, with love and reassurance.

"Darling Girl, everyone's life has to end. I'm not afraid to die. We have had a loving life not many people are lucky enough to know. I couldn't have had a better life if I had been a king. I'm so grateful for every moment.

"Do you know what I would like to do? I want to talk to Allan Peterkin. I'd like to see if he would say a thanksgiving mass for me. Not a laying on of hands, or prayers for some miraculous recovery . . . none of that. A mass of thanksgiving just for you, the children, Glen and Christopher and Julian, Bill and his family . . . . really just family and a few close friends, the Lewises and the Falconers."

And so it was on Friday, September 19 we all

gathered at the Jesuits' Bellarmine Residence for a thanksgiving service in which each of us took a part. In some ways it was an unlikely group: my sister Pat and Aunt Mildred, who are Baptist by upbringing and lifelong conviction; our dear friends, the Lewises, who are Jewish (Hy's part of the service was from the Old Testament); the Falconers, who are Anglican; our children, who have been brought up associated with the United Church; and Bill and Mary's family, who are devout Roman Catholics. But Allan Peterkin, a friend and a Jesuit, is a wise as well as godly man who understands that spiritual values and approaches to God do not necessarily need neat labels.

The service took a half-hour and truly was one of thanksgiving. It concluded with Gerhard and me at the altar reading the one verse together

My Dear People
Let us love one another
Since Love comes from God
And everyone who loves is begotten by God and
    knows God
And anyone who fails to love can never have
    known God
For God is Love.

Allan gave us communion. It was a half-hour

which drew us all close to one another in a deep spiritual sense. Afterwards everyone came back to our home for a roast beef dinner that is something of a tradition at the Kennedys.

In all these days now there is an underlying sense of urgency, of files to be straightened, work to be completed if possible, wills to be drawn up, and hard realistic details to be faced.

Gerhard is now on weekly doses of 5FU, our one slim hope about which we have few illusions. Our doctor has explained that this drug fights a rearguard action against cancer of the liver in about 25 per cent of the cases, sometimes effecting a remission. It is not a cure. Even if it does buy some time, the cancer regroups its forces and eventually takes over again. At its very best the drug may delay the inevitable. At its worst it may do nothing more than cause unpleasant side effects. For a couple of days after each treatment Gerhard is really low physically.

But he does not give in, and our days are busy. Shawn has come home from B.C. and is chauffeuring Gerhard on his business calls. Our family dinners, always special events in the days, now, take on a new and special meaning. Glen, Chris, and Julian make it a point to drop in frequently. We have always been a closely-knit family and the closeness is doubly important now.

Gerhard and I often talk far into the night, sometimes about our earlier life together, sometimes about our thought of the present. And then there is the future, which must be faced.

"I've been thinking where I would like to be buried," Gerhard said thoughtfully one morning. "Not up the street. Not somewhere that is surrounded by subways and traffic and city noises."

I wondered if he would like to be buried out west, since he had been born and raised in Winnipeg.

"No . . . there is no reason to be buried there."

We explored the idea of the North Shore of Lake Superior, that magnificent country we had travelled and camped in together with Tracy, Shawn, and Maureen, Gerhard's granddaughter. Those days on the North Shore had been wondrous days of discovery and deep contentment, in country for which Gerhard felt a kinship and sense of belonging. But the wilderness nature of that shore was the very thing that made the idea impractical.

"What about the Gatineau Hills?" he suggested. "They are very special to you, part of your childhood, part of your life. We have all the memories of our times there with our children. It's a place you would like to go back to." Gerhard was thinking it through aloud.

Of course. It all seemed right.

"It's the place I would want to be buried, too. . . . right beside you," I confirmed the idea.

We decided to go to Ottawa that weekend. Hy had loaned us his larger car, which was more comfortable for Gerhard, since he could stretch out across the back seat and rest. Shawn drove us, and in Ottawa we picked up Mildred, who had made some enquiries for us, and then set out for the Gatineau.

We found what was right in every way in a small, old cemetery atop a hill. A narrow gravel road followed a stream, went past a mill and waterfall, across a small bridge, then bearing to the right, the road ran up a hill, and there, on top, was the cemetery. Along one side, lovely open woods with outcroppings of granite seemed to stand sentinel over the little graveyard. In some directions you looked out across the rolling hills and valleys, and, in another, down towards the Gatineau River. It was a September day when Gerhard and I stood there together, and those hills have never looked more splendid and beautiful in autumn colour.

It could sound morbid. But it was anything but

a morbid day. It was a happy one. It was a uniquely personal shared experience, and it brought us a kind of knowledge about what our final chapter would be. There is no way to explain our feelings: in fact we marvelled at them ourselves. We both felt happy.

So we were dismayed when we found on enquiries that you could not simply go and make arrangements for a family plot. Precisely because the cemetery was so small and in such a lovely location there were strict by-laws governing the availability of plots.

We talked with Homer Cross and William Caves, treasurer and chairman of the local committee. We explained that our need was an almost immediate one, and talked in great detail of our long connection with the area, which of the family in the past had owned property in the Gatineau. . . . And they heard us with sympathy and understanding.

It was late Sunday afternoon when we started back for Toronto with assurances from Mr. Caves and Mr. Cross that they would bring our request before the committee and let us know their decision.

As soon as we got home that night I sat up in bed beside Gerhard and penned notes to both men. The little cemetery in the Gatineau had become terribly important to us. To know we would be buried there side by side had become our most important objective ... something which meant a sense of completion, a sense of going home. A few months ago I would not have believed that there could be these emotions on such a matter of finality.

Gerhard and I talked of it within the family circle, describing every aspect of the place and locale. The children, seeing how much this meant to us, were optimistic and encouraging.

At dinner that Monday night the phone rang and it was Mr. Cross to tell us that the committee had given its unanimous approval to our application. Gerhard and I expressed our gratitude and promised to go back the next weekend to make final arrangements. We chose places next to the woods, with Gerhard's burial place directly beneath an enormous windswept pine tree, and mine right alongside.

That weekend we also asked a local monument-maker to seek out a selection of granite rocks from the area as we would like headstones that were natural, uncut save for our names. We would decide when we saw what he came up with if we should use one stone marker for the two of us, or separate ones. He was to call us when he found something and we would come back to make a choice. We had made two long trips to Ottawa and were prepared to make one more to complete the arrangements. To us these details were important.

We were discovering that death is the most personal matter of all — much more intimate than birth.

Many times we spoke of our sense of pleasure and peace at our Gatineau Hills purchase. And it was in one of those moments that Gerhard spoke to me seriously and earnestly about the years ahead for me.

"Darling Girl, you'll have much of your life still ahead of you. I hope you won't live it alone. You won't be able to think of it now. But in the years to come there may be someone else, someone you will love. Not as you and I love one another, but someone you'll share something different with. It might even turn out that the Gatineau arrangements we have made will not seem right for you when the time comes. And if that should happen I would not want you to feel guilty. It would be all right."

His words brought home the enormity of death. I told him my life was so centred and involved with him that there was no room for any other thought, that I found comfort in knowing my burial place was right alongside his, and that I could only live in the now, with him right here, as honestly and openly as we had all our lives. Even facing his own death, his concern was for me.

That night, lying in his arms, I suggested that we both just pack up our work and spend every minute together. Gerhard wouldn't hear of it. He felt there were too many things he wanted to do and that my work was going to be necessary for me in the future.

It was one of the lowest moments for me. I could taste the emptiness there would be without him. I found myself panicking. I have always loved life, run towards it eagerly much as Gerhard does, savouring every moment, even the painful ones. But that night I examined the thought of ending my life with his. What if we were to take some pills, wrap our arms around one another, and simply go to sleep, never to wake up.

It was the only thought in all those long weeks of Gerhard's illness that I did not share with him. I knew too well what his reaction would have been. He would have been angry, insulted, above all disappointed in me. And at the core of my being, I knew that I could do no such thing. The thought was born of the blind panic of the moment. . . that's all.

Home

OCTOBER came and the lovely autumn days looked as though they could go on forever. It was one of the mildest, most beautiful autumns on record. Gerhard continued to work; there were several deadlines he was trying to meet. Two air-supported structures were scheduled for erection and he was coping with the details and frustrations that seem part of so much business. I had trimmed my work load of most extra commitments, the one exception being a government committee to review provincial spending. Since there were only three members from the private sector and the complex work was so far under way as to make a replacement impossible, I compromised and left the meetings at 4:00 P.M. in order to be home when Gerhard came home. The minutes and hours with him were the most important thing in my life.

Some people live their lives in tight little knots of anxiety, their eyes and minds darting birdlike to pick critically at everything and everyone around them. The sharper their knife-thrust, the greater their satisfaction. Cut someone else down and increase your own stature. It's a way of life. Gerhard was just the opposite. He had no need to belittle anyone. I think he was truly a whole person and because he was, the accomplishments of others gave him pleasure. He could afford to be generous in spirit, and he was.

In mid-October we talked with Agnes, his former wife, and asked if she would like to come east, with his mother, for a visit. We knew the going would get rough as time went on, and it seemed better to have that visit accomplished while Gerhard was still well enough to make it a happy occasion. His brother Bill made the arrangements.

Time and geography had drawn three of Gerhard's four older children increasingly into our orbit, while the fourth was with UNICEF in Pakistan. Because we saw so much of Glen, and at other times of young Gerhard and Nancy, in recent years we had made it a habit to keep in touch with Agnes and in some measure try to share family events and news. This rather odd arrangement couldn't have come about except for the kind of person Gerhard was, and the place his children found in our home and life. After years of no contact at all, Agnes and I had become friends.

So Agnes and Mother Kennedy came for their visit and that was one more pleasant duty accomplished. Mother thought Gerhard looked fine, and we saw no reason to disturb her with harsh realities that would come along soon enough. There were the Van Moles of Swan Lake hunting days and Gerhard phoned them to say his farewells. Sadly, there was not the hoped-for opportunity for a farewell visit with old and valued hunting and fishing friends from St. Paul.

Meanwhile there were some undercurrents at home that kept surfacing. Gerhard would sometimes stop in mid-sentence in the course of a phone conversation with Glen or Bill. Something was going on. Gerhard told me he was planning a surprise for me, but it was taking him some time to get all the bits and pieces together. When he mentioned that

Don McEachern and Bill Baker were putting some of his film sound track on cartridge I began to suspect that the surprise was some kind of sound and visual compilation.

Whatever the surprise was to be, it was evident that he was getting great pleasure out of planning it. And if the secretive phone calls were any indication, he was busy about that surprise at least part of every day. For once, my own natural curiosity was quiescent. My concerns were all for Gerhard.

Gerhard had always had great shoulders and arms, a deep chest and leg muscles like bands of steel. He had been an outdoor person all his life, capable, assured, competent in many areas. But now the cancer had eroded most of the muscle tissue, till his arms were now little larger than my own, and bones were almost all that was left of his shoulders, hips, and thighs.

Now it was I who gathered him in my arms, wishing with all my heart that I could give him my strength. While all the lovely muscle disappeared cruelly, his abdomen grew swollen, tender, and painful, as the liver acted out its protest.

But don't for a moment get a picture of a man who had given up. He never did. On Friday, October 24, Gerhard had invited our close friends the Lewises and Falconers, and Bill and Mary to join the family for dinner. He had notes at the table for Jim, Hy, Bill, and Christopher, notes of personal thanks for their love and friendship over the years. And at my place sat a little package with a ribbon attached.

With Gerhard gaily directing the proceedings I followed the ribbon to the front door, out the door, across the lawn to the driveway — and there was the car he had planned for me with such loving care. He had even arranged spotlights on the garage roof that were trained on the car. Inside the car he had included every imaginable feature you could want, and he showed me each and every one so proudly and with such boyish pleasure that I thought my heart would break. Am/Fm radio, tape deck. Yes, there was the tape with the music from the films he had produced.

There was a note in Gerhard's bold, firm hand, beginning "Beloved Girl: These keys unlock your very own Grenada Ghia" and telling something of its special details. He wrote that Bill had offered to keep the car in mint condition "like the aura that has always surrounded our life together". We took our first ride in the car that very night, driving Bill and Mary home. It was a delight to drive. Next day we used it for a trip out of town to oversee the erection of one of the air-supported structures. It was a long day and a tiring one. Gerhard was grey with exhaustion when we got home, but terribly pleased that the bubble was up. It was ironic that several years of hard work were just now coming together with exciting results, just as Gerhard's life was ebbing. Yet he never once complained or suggested that there was any unfairness in these circumstances. There was not an ounce of bitterness in him.

That night as we got into bed we both remarked how swollen his feet and ankles were. Next day they were no better. In fact the swelling seemed to be working its way up the legs. By Sunday, when bed rest and keeping his feet elevated did not seem to be helping, we called the doctor, who prescribed a diuretic.

After taking the medication Gerhard was back and forth to the bathroom with great frequency. Then he began to have real pain. We believed he was having a reaction to the medication and that it would gradually wear off. When that did not happen we called the doctor the next day and went down to Princess Margaret Hospital.

Hospital

WHEN Dr. Rider saw Gerhard he wondered why we had waited so long. He told us that Gerhard was in real trouble. Phone conversations went back and forth between him and Dr. David Smith, and finally word came that there was a hospital room for him immediately. I took Gerhard to Toronto Western Hospital. It was October 28.

At this point a specialist in urology took over and he and David kept us well informed during the uphill battle. No one ever fooled us about the long-term prospects. But there was a period where we were all hopeful that things could be brought under enough control that Gerhard would be able to get home again.

It's worth mentioning that in all these months Gerhard had never asked for nor accepted any suggestion that pain killers might be useful. He wanted to be fully aware in whatever time of living was left to him.

Those first few days I would leave the house just after 7:00 A.M.; visit with Gerhard before going to the studio for 9:45; return to the hospital for a noon visit; and go back again after my radio show ended at 4:00 P.M. At the radio station Mac McCurdy and Don Hartford told me to take whatever time I needed. But for the moment I needed the stability of my work responsibilities. I needed the deadlines, with their demands, to keep me from falling to pieces, which would have helped neither Gerhard nor our children. And with the help of Irene Wilson Domnas, my program assistant, the deadlines were met.

At home Tracy asked if she could sleep with me. And did.

Sometimes Gerhard would still be asleep when I arrived at the hospital first thing in the morning and

I would leave a note close to his hand. One morning I brought him a longer note to keep with him while I was at the studio.

Oct. 31, 1975.

My Beloved Man:

How many times in these last few weeks have I said "I love you"? How small are the words for the world of meaning they have.

They mean: I can see you clearly, still, as you were that first evening across the room at a party I had no idea I would go to. They hold the excitement of that evening and the many that followed . . . our times together in the Gatineau, the Laurentians, New York, Chicago.

They mean: the marvellous mystery of our passion — insatiable and yet so often so fully satisfied. . . the most complete giving, that replenishes and enriches beyond all power to describe.

And the words mean: thank you for our beautiful children, each such a distinct and unique individual. I cannot imagine any other person whose children I would rather have had.

And they mean: thank you for being the most remarkable man you are. You embody strength, compassion, excitement, the excitement not only of passion, but that of the visionary man-of-ideas who sees endless possibilities in everything around him. You are so much of life to me, my Darling. Remember our visit to the Whiteshell? The rain and sleet that froze against our clothes that late afternoon in the marsh? You have always made me believe anything is possible; you have given me a strength and courage and confidence in living. I admire you and respect you so deeply, my dearest, for you really do know how to live.

All of these things, and so many more are there, in those words, "I love you."

You are most of life to me — and that will never change.

You have my love, always — in this life, and whatever comes after.

Betty

He kept that note close at hand for days and once was quite upset when it slipped off the bed and wasn't within reach.

Shawn, who had returned to B.C., now came flying home. Mark, who had planned for a year to go to Germany on a long-term basis to become fluent in German for his doctorate in philosophy, cancelled his plans. Nancy came east to be with the family and her Dad. Glen and Christopher, in the middle of closing the purchase of a new farm, were back and forth to the hospital. Ill as Gerhard was, he sat and talked excitedly with Chris for well over an hour one evening planning with him the future studio in one of the great barns at the new farm. He still generated enthusiasm and a marvellous zest for a new project, even someone else's.

He was still trying to work from his hospital bed, and our youngest son, D'Arcy, was pitching in to follow through with the outside work for his Dad.

Gerhard had a catheter in and was on intravenous feeding. The urology specialist explained that a prostate operation offered the only possibility of getting Gerhard off the catheter. If that could be accomplished, perhaps there was a chance he could get home.

The real question was whether or not Gerhard could even stand the anaesthetic necessary for the prostate procedure. We waited a few days, and finally the decision was made to go ahead.

Gerhard went into surgery at 8:00 A.M. and was not back from the recovery room until late afternoon. My sister Pat, a nurse, specialed him that first night. For the next ten days and nights I stayed beside Gerhard, never leaving the hospital. There was no thought of work, or home, or anything but Gerhard. Mark and Shawn took turns staying at the hospital all night. I think they felt that if Dad died they wanted to be sure I was not left there alone.

When the urology specialist discovered me sleeping on a couple of chairs one night, he went off and got a stretcher and brought that in. From then on I slept nights beside Gerhard, on that stretcher.

November 16 was Tracy's thirteenth birthday and we tried to celebrate it with Gerhard with a candlelit cake and ice cream in his room. It all fell flat when Gerhard proved too sick that evening to enjoy cake or company, and we were all saddened by watching him make the effort.

November 18 was to have been a red letter day for us: my first meeting as a member of the board of directors of the Bank of Montreal. How pleased and proud Gerhard was of that appointment. Now Gerhard wanted me to make the trip to Montreal, but I felt there was only one place I could be, there beside him. He even spoke to David about it, in front of me, asking David to insist that I go. David told him quietly, "Gerhard, this is where Betty should be now." And we did not discuss it further. I sent my apologies and received a touching personal note from the Chairman.

Gerhard began to bleed internally and there

seemed very little we could do but wait. He was being given blood and was on intravenous. In all this time he was conscious, clear-headed. Many times I just sat touching him, holding his hand. And many times he would say, "I'm so lucky to have you. I wouldn't want to be going through this without you." Eventually the bleeding stopped and we breathed easier again.

We have enough family that there was often someone besides me with Gerhard. And when our family and David began to express concern for my health if I didn't spend some hours out of that hospital room, I reluctantly went back to work, leaving the hospital about 9:30 each morning and returning at 4:30 to spend the nights with Gerhard. And I phoned several times during the hours I was downtown.

Meanwhile, my sister and the boys kept things going at home for Tracy.

The nurses on the tenth floor, under the remarkably kind and competent Miss Brown, were consistently helpful and caring. With so many Kennedys coming and going, I'm sure the very presence of so much family complicated their lives, but they never made us feel anything but welcome.

Perhaps it was Gerhard himself who had much

to do with their response. I remember one nurse dropping something in the bathroom with a terrible clatter. Gerhard's innate courtesy came through, even through his desperate illness. He automatically called out in concern, "Can I help you with anything?"

Adventure

THERE was a timelessness about those days and nights. You couldn't tell if a minute, an hour, or an eternity had passed. There was the strength of the family melded together, each offering the other loving support, and that was precious and necessary.

Allan Peterkin, our Jesuit friend, offered to perform whatever service we would wish, and suggested a church that would be suitable. Gerhard and I were easy and secure in our minds about the Gatineau Hills for burial. As for a service, Gerhard had expressly said that he wanted no "big fuss with a casket rolling down the aisles". In fact, when we had spoken of this earlier, he had said that he saw no reason for a service in Toronto at all, but rather at the graveside only. I had told him there would be many friends who would like a chance to honour him, and we should plan a memorial service for Toronto.

And so Allan, Bill, our sons, and I planned that service for Gerhard, making it as personal and individual and loving as we could. Our three sons, and Gerhard Jr., and Christopher and Hy would each take part. Shawn specified that he would write whatever he would say at that service when the time came, rather than select any other reading.

As the late November days came we did not need to hear the doctors tell us that they were amazed at Gerhard's strength and endurance. The lack of a properly functioning liver was causing all sorts of unpleasant side-effects. Gerhard's abdomen was distended. One leg was swollen so hard and tight it must have been painful for him simply to bear the weight. And now they did tell him to say when he was uncomfortable, for there was no point in him suffering needlessly.

Gerhard's two sisters, one from Chicago, the

other from Winnipeg, came to see him. And when young Gerhard, a jet pilot Major in the forces flew in from Cold Lake, Alberta, to see his father it was a very emotional time. Both knew that they would not see one another again. When Tony, Gerhard's second son by his earlier marriage, phoned from Pakistan where he is with UNICEF, even a poor connection could not spoil Gerhard's pleasure in the call. He lay back on his pillow and said with a smile, "Now I've spoken to them all."

There had been a call from the monument-maker in Ottawa, and one morning I slipped down there by plane. Mildred picked me up at the airport and we went to see the stones that had been select-ed. All taken right from the cemetery site in the hills, there were three granite rocks, two small ones and one larger. The larger, single stone was my choice, as I felt that our lives were so much of one piece. I asked that our names and birth dates be chiselled into the granite, and that it be placed as soon as completed at the cemetery in Wakefield. The monument-maker suggested the addition of one small ancient symbol on the rock . . . one which symbolized the mysterious union of man and wom-an. He had never used it before, but thought it appropriate for us. I agreed.

Some days later I told Gerhard what I had done.

He listened carefully and then asked me to tell it all to him again. I told him that our stone would be there, in place, with both our names on it. He was quiet and thoughtful, and squeezed my hand tightly. There was no need for words.

Gerhard was sleeping more of the time, now, and some pain killers were becoming necessary to keep him comfortable. But when he was awake he was fully aware; he carried on conversations with us and wanted me near.

On Saturday, November 22 there were several of us with him in the evening . . . Shawn, Glen and Chris, Nancy, and I. Gerhard was sitting up and we were talking about a variety of things.

There was a lull and Gerhard sat there looking around at each of us. . . . "Some very strange things are happening," he said. "I don't know if I can find the words to explain it. I am so conscious of all of your love around me. But it's not the way I have known your love all my life. It's quite different. It's as though everything comes all together in one thing." He looked thoughtful . . . as though these words just weren't conveying what he wanted to say.

Shawn said, "I know, Dad. You see, you are the catalyst. . . . You are in each of us and what comes back to you is yourself, you and us. . . ."

Gerhard looked intently at Shawn . . . our Shawn

who always has been trying to explain unexplainable things, and said ... "Shawn knows. ... Shawn knows. ... What I am trying to say is ... I am not sad. This is an adventure. And the physical things are just a nuisance."

Gerhard could not have given us a greater gift. He shared his own peace with us.

The last week of November Allan Peterkin asked if he might come and give us both communion. He came along with Bill and Bill's young son Danny, who had just made his first communion. There was nothing grim or foreboding about what I assume were "the last rites".

As we entered December, Gerhard's strength diminished further. Several of us now stayed the night at the hospital, cat-napping on chairs in Gerhard's room and the small reception room down the hall. Wednesday, December 3 was a long and anxious night. Thursday, December 4, about 8:00 A.M. Mark stayed at his father's side while the rest of us went downstairs for a quick breakfast. I couldn't wait till the others were finished; I felt a sense of urgency to get back, close to Gerhard, and went upstairs again. Mark said he was glad I had come right back, he didn't like the sound of Dad's breathing.

Gerhard opened his eyes, reached out for me and with a strength it seemed impossible for him to possess, enclosed me tightly in his arms. I put my arms under him and we clung to one another. "I love you. I love you," he said, and I told him I loved him, forever. And then he simply stopped breathing.

Aftermath

THAT afternoon Gordon Sinclair had this to say about Gerhard, in a radio broadcast:

Gerhard Kennedy, whom I've known for almost twenty years, was a visionary, a man of soaring imagination in terms of the future, a man of courage and love of nature.

His vision encompassed abstract things like protection of the environment and wild life; practical things such as improved transportation and quick construction in times of emergency or for temporary use.

Many buildings needed for a short time are built in the style and the costly method of a generation ago at the very least. Gerhard Kennedy had ideas, some of them in daily use right now, for temporary buildings to meet transient needs.

In conversation with him, the person *without* robust imagination might reel as if punch drunk from the flood of words covering new ways of doing old things.

Gerhard had an eye for beauty . . . indeed he made a movie about the artistic Group of Seven and had A. Y. Jackson, dean of that school, in his preview audience.

He saw the food and shelter possibilities of climate control in the Arctic or sub-Arctic and did a picture about that too.

Once I was with him in a spot of Ontario forest that had long stood unmarked by the passage of human feet even though it was within seventy miles of Toronto. Gerhard looked around at fallen branches, rotting stumps, and broken boughs and almost put me into a state of trance by telling how this fallen vegetation could be used for value without disturbing the wilderness theme.

His love of the outdoors . . . and his evidence of courage was shown in his personal selection of his last resting place.

Several weeks ago when Gerhard still had the strength but knew it could not endure, he and Betty went into the Gatineau Hills and selected a burial spot. That takes a measure of realism that few people have and yet, to repeat, Gerhard Kennedy was a man of vision. The perception included his own death which he described to his family as a new experience. An experience that comes to all.

His home, shared with Betty, his sons and daughter, backed on the Humber River, and Gerhard got to know the river by its sound; the roar of spring, the occasional crack of winter, the whisper of summer, and the cry of marine birds.

My own house is on the next creek to the west, so I could share his feelings about the changing seasons as revealed by the waters. The houses being in line with the airport further west meant that Gerhard would drive Betty to my place and pick me up when we went on out-of-town appearances for "Front Page Challenge". On those drives his imagination was always ranging over this problem or that solution; this new way of handling a situation or that analysis of the way things could be.

Our last non-Toronto assignment was to Windsor, and even though he was weaker and paler than before, Gerhard came to the airport. The only difference was that this time one of his sons did the driving. He was animated as usual and bright of eye.

When Betty and her son went inside to check luggage and confirm departure time and gate, Gerhard and I stood in knowledgeable conversation. It was the last time we were to see each other and perhaps both of us knew this to be the situation. It was not the last time we *spoke*, there being occasional telephone communications in which I did the duty bit, knowing what the answer would be.

"Anything I can get you; anything you need?"

The answer was always the same. "Everything is fine; no problems, nothing needed here. I've got more of everything than I need."

The strain must have been very hard on Betty, just as was similar strain on Norma Dennett a few months ago. It must be difficult for them to atune to the realization that they are widows; victims of the same enemy in the same year.

But since we live on in our children, neither man is really gone. One of the Dennett girls looks just like Norma, another looks just like Jack. The Kennedy boys have a way of talking, the angle of the mouth, the position of the watching eyes. This is Gerhard we are seeing in the sons. The stream of life rolls on.

Gordon Sinclair

That same day the *Toronto Star* obituary sketched the outline of his life:

Gerhard Kennedy, fashion designer, film-maker, and manufacturer of "air bubble" enclosures for recreational and industrial use, died in hospital today. He was 63.

Kennedy, of Old Mill Rd., was associated with his wife, broadcaster Betty Kennedy, in Kennedy Horizons Ltd., a company producing educational films.

Born in Winnipeg, he attended the University of Wisconsin. He entered his father's firm, Northern Shirt Co., and set up Gerhard Kennedy (Canada) Ltd. His sportswear sold to top retailers in Canada and the U.S. In 1953 he was chosen to represent Canada for special coronation fashions along with such internationally known firms as Dior, Fath, and Amies.

Manitoba Open golf champion in 1943, Kennedy sponsored one of the first major golf tournaments with a $10,000 prize which drew Ben Hogan and Sam Snead. He was named to the advisory council of the Professional Golfers Association of America.

For a while Kennedy represented Schenley Distilleries for Western Canada and rose to national sales manager. After his resignation in 1957, he spent almost three years trying to establish a national wildlife conservation foundation.

Kennedy met his present wife, the former Betty Styran of Ottawa, when both were working in the fashion industry.

He is survived by four children by his first wife, Major Gerhard Kennedy, Jr. of Cold Lake, Alta., Anthony, in Pakistan with UNICEF, Nancy Clare of Winnipeg, and Glen Chapman of Markham, and four from his second marriage, Mark of Toronto, Shawn of Goldbridge, B.C., and D'Arcy and Tracy of Toronto.

A memorial service will be held tomorrow at 4 p.m. in St. Joan of Arc Church, Bloor St. W. Interment will be in the Gatineau Hills, at Wakefield, Que.

That Friday Allan Peterkin, S.J. conducted the memorial service for Gerhard in St. Joan of Arc Church on Bloor Street. We had selected every part of that service specially for Gerhard.

Allan conducted the mass with D'Arcy and Gerhard Jr. assisting. Hy Lewis, Gerhard's oldest friend read the beautiful "Psalm of David". From *The Prophet*, which Gerhard and I have both loved for years, Chris read the passage on Religion and Mark read the passage on Death.

And Shawn stood straight and tall and in a clear, calm voice read from his own personal notebook.

I am sitting in a room with my father, a man whom I have known for all of the twenty-four years of my life. He will remain a strength and a beacon for the rest of my life. Some of you have known him longer than I, and have shared in his life in other ways. Certainly, no one could have really known him without having come to love him — because this was the feeling that characterized his relationship with his friends, family, and the world that surrounded him.

His tremendous capacity to enjoy life was reflected by his artistic nature, as he sought to express the beauty he saw in this world. This expression took many forms, examples being films and paintings. A memory I have is of my father asking for the stump of an apple tree that had been cut down next door, then proceeding to labour with great affection, preserving the foundation of that tree as a base for a table which is still in our yard.

To be able to share the life he lived and to communicate the discoveries that his interest in everything uncovered were of utmost importance. He was very successful in these endeavours, as life provided him with the ability to do this, as well as a wealth of experience to draw from. Perhaps the most unusual and marked quality of this man was his ability to recognize the achievements of others and encourage the growth of all who knew him.

There was never the all-too-common feeling that his own person would be shaded by the accomplishments of another.

Near the end of his life all of his family came

to surround him — and to realize the great love we feel for him and each other. It seems a fitting tribute to him that he should be the catalyst for such a bonding of his family.

He saw his own death as an adventure, knowing it as an inevitable part of human life. He never lost this feeling, nor did he shift his concern from those he would leave behind to himself at any time.

I feel that discoveries and revelations came to him as such a full life drew to a close.

Several of the family have commented on the indescribable feeling of spending time with Gerhard during the past few weeks, and of the strange timelessness felt in his presence.

I am happy for him now, as he becomes more than ever a part of this earth and the force that gives life and movement to existence here.

As I write this it is apparent to me that his life is not ended, but changed.

Shawn Kennedy

So many people have since remarked on that service, how it carried such a feeling of hope and thankfulness. I am glad. It was meant to.

An old friend, George Boukydis, took charge of all the arrangements at the house after the service. So many people came . . . so many with their support and kindness. . . . Both then, and later in letters and notes and comments, friends and even strangers offered their sympathy. There is a force in the feelings of others that comforts and sustains. It is a real thing. And it helps.

Early Saturday morning we set out to drive to Ottawa. Now it was just immediate family, and Allan Peterkin, who came as a family friend. In Ottawa we were joined by more family and began the drive out of Ottawa up the Gatineau to Wakefield.

Gerhard and I had earlier decided that as much as possible the local people at Wakefield should look after our arrangements. The Reverend Thomas Simms, the United Church minister there, had agreed to conduct the burial service, and he was there to meet us, as was the kindly Mr. Caves who had been so helpful in our obtaining our family plot.

Gerhard was buried beneath that beautiful old pine tree, just as we had talked about it standing there together in September. Our stone, just plain natural granite, is there, in place, with both our names on it.

For me those moments at the graveside were softened, and less painful than they would have been, because we had planned every step of the way together. It didn't seem so desolate somehow. And the Minister's words, "home is the hunter, to a place of rest", seemed fitting, complete, good. And I have such a sense of Gerhard with me.

The months of illness, the hospital time, the long anxious nights, those were not the hard part. Those we shared. With my hand in Gerhard's we could face anything. This is the hard part. Now. Without him.

I have never known anyone in all my life, so completely unafraid of life . . . even the ending of it, which he saw as yet another adventure.

My beloved Gerhard has left me a legacy of strength, courage, and pure wonder at life. And that will help me to survive.